God's Goodness, Gifts & Grace

Susan Leffler

Written and Illustrated by Susan Leffler
Inspired by the Holy Spirit

Scripture taken from the New King James Version.
Copyright 1982 by Thomas Nelson, Inc.
Used by permission.
All rights reserved.

Hi, my name is Grace but everyone calls me Gracie. This is Oscar my puppy. I want to tell you about God and how good He is and all of His special gifts He has for you.

A long time ago God created the heavens and the earth. But before He created Adam and Eve, He made sure everything they would ever need was here on the earth first.

You see the earth was all water in the beginning, so if God put Adam and Eve here first before He created the land and the plants and the trees, they would have been doing a lot of swimming!

But God knew what they needed. They would need the land to live on, the plants and trees to provide food and shelter, the sun to provide warmth and light during the day and the moon to give them light at night. And of course God gave them His love! God will provide everything you need, just like He did with Adam and Eve because God is good!

The earth was without form, and void; and darkness was on the face of the deep.
And the Spirit of God was hovering over the face of the waters.

Gen 1:2

And God said, "See, I have given you every herb that yields seed which is on
the face of all the earth, and every tree whose fruit yields seed; to you it shall be for food.

Gen 1:29

He loves righteousness and justice; The earth is full of the goodness of the LORD.

Psalm 33:5

He causes the grass to grow for the cattle, and vegetation for the service of man,
that he may bring forth food from the earth.

Psalm 104:14

God also gave you free will.
That means you can make your own choices.
Adam and Eve had free will and were able to make
their own choices. But one day Eve listened to a voice
that was not God's and she made the wrong choice.

There are a lot of choices you have to make in life.

Now the serpent was more cunning than any beast of the field which the LORD God had made. And he said to the woman, "Has God indeed said, 'You shall not eat of every tree of the garden'?"

Gen 3:1

And the LORD God said to the woman, "What is this you have done?"
The woman said, "The serpent deceived me, and I ate."

Gen 3:13

"That you may love the LORD your God, that you may obey His voice, and that you may cling to Him, for He is your life and the length of your days…"

Deut 30.20

And there are consequences in the choices you make...
good and bad!

O God, You know my foolishness; And my sins are not hidden from You.

Psalm 69.5

Do not be deceived, God is not mocked; for whatever a man sows, that he will also reap.

Gal 6:7

God has nothing but the best for you.
God wants to spend time with you
like He did with Adam and Eve in the garden.

God is your friend and your teacher and
He will lead you into all things that are good
because He is good.

Trust in the LORD with all your heart, and lean not on your own understanding;
In all your ways acknowledge Him, and He shall direct your paths.

Prov 3:5,6

For I know the thoughts that I think toward you, says the LORD,
thoughts of peace and not of evil, to give you a future and a hope.

Jer 29:11

"Now therefore, listen to me, my children, for blessed are those who keep my ways.
Hear instruction and be wise, and do not disdain it.

Prov 8:32,33

Oh, how great is Your goodness, which You have laid up for those who fear You,
Which You have prepared for those who trust in You in the presence of the sons of men!

Psalm 31:19

The goodness of God comes through His love for you, for me, for the whole world! Because of one man, Adam, and his disobedience, sin came into the world. God loved us so much that He knew He would have to save us from all sin, so He sent His most precious gift to us, His Son Jesus.

"For God so loved the world that He gave His only begotten Son, that whoever believes in Him should not perish but have everlasting life.

John 3:16

So by one man, Jesus, all our sins, all our sickness and disease, all our sorrows and pain, all that sin brought into this world, that one man, Jesus, took it all upon His own body on the cross. Jesus died for us. But Jesus rose from the dead and sits at the right hand of God. He defeated death. Jesus won for us!

But thanks be to God, who gives us the victory through our Lord Jesus Christ.

1 Cor 15:57

For as by one man's disobedience many were made sinners, so also by one Man's obedience many will be made righteous.

Rom 5:19

He will swallow up death forever, and the Lord GOD will wipe away tears from all faces...

Isa 25:8

Surely, He has borne our griefs and carried our sorrows....But He was wounded for our transgressions, He was bruised for our iniquities; the chastisement for our peace was upon Him and by His stripes we are healed.

Isa 53:4,5

When you receive God's most precious gift, His Son Jesus
into your heart, you receive the gift of salvation.
And that includes healing, prosperity,
forgiveness of all your sins, past, present and future
and you have eternal life with Papa God!

That if you confess with your mouth the Lord Jesus and believe in your heart that God
has raised Him from the dead, you will be saved. For with the heart one believes
unto righteousness, and with the mouth confession is made unto salvation.
Rom 10:9,10

You become a son or a daughter of Almighty God by believing
and putting your faith in what Jesus did for you on the cross.
And Papa God loves to give His children gifts! It's like your birthday!
But these gifts are special and precious and will last forever!

Behold what manner of love the Father has bestowed on us, that we should be called children of God!
1 John 3:1

Every good gift and every perfect gift is from above, and comes down from the Father of lights, with whom there is no variation or shadow of turning.

James 1:17

"Do not fear, little flock, for it is your Father's good pleasure to give you the kingdom.

Luke 12:32

The day you ask Jesus into your heart you get all the fruits of His Spirit and that's all good stuff because Jesus is all good.

Jesus described it like this; that He is the vine and you are the branch. When the branch is attached to the vine the branch will produce good fruit.Jesus produced the fruit of love, joy, peace, patience, kindness, goodness, gentleness, faith and self-control.

These fruits are the true character of Jesus. He gives these of Himself because He is good, they are for you. The more you practice and use these gifts God has given you, the more you grow into the person God created you to be. Not only you and I, but everyone, needs all of these qualities to be a better person…to be more like Jesus!

But the fruit of the Spirit is love, joy, peace, longsuffering, kindness, goodness, faithfulness, gentleness, self-control.

Gal 5:22,23

Let no one despise your youth, but be an example to the believers in word, in conduct, in love, in spirit, in faith, in purity.

1 Tim 4:12

"I am the vine, you are the branches. He who abides in Me, and I in him, bears much fruit; for without Me you can do nothing.

John 15:5

God will also give you gifts that are to be used for others.
These are spiritual gifts and are to be used to help people
who may have a problem or are sick and hurting or
just need a word from God to encourage them.

The gifts that God gives you are to be used.
They are not to be forgotten and put away like
some of your old toys in the back of your closet.

As each one has received a gift, minister it to one another,
as good stewards of the manifold grace of God.

1 Peter 4:10

But the manifestation of the Spirit is given to each one for the profit of all: for to one is given
the word of wisdom... to another the word of knowledge... to another faith... gifts of healings...
to another the working of miracles, to another prophecy, to another discerning of spirits,
to another different kinds of tongues, to another the interpretation of tongues. But one and
the same Spirit works all these things, distributing to each one individually as He wills.

1 Cor 12:7-11

Do not neglect the gift that is in you, which was given to you by prophecy with the laying on of
the hands of the eldership.

1 Tim 4:14

God gives us gifts you can't see with your eyes.
But He gave you faith to believe in them.
When you put these gifts into practice, others will see these gifts
and know God is real and He is here and He is good.

I asked God, "Who should I give these toys to Papa?"
He said, "Give the doll to Anna and tell her I love her."

"Give the ball and bat to Frankie and tell him to practice
and he will be good at all he sets his hands to."

"And give the ball to Timothy, for he has a playful and joyful heart."

I told each of them what God told me and they all left knowing
they had a word from God and that God loved them.
Bless others with the gifts God gives you and you will be blessed too!

…while we do not look at the things which are seen, but at the things which are not seen.
For the things which are seen are temporary, but the things which are not seen are eternal.
2 Cor 4:18

For the gifts and the calling of God are irrevocable.
Rom 11:29

Meditate on these things; give yourself entirely to them, that your progress may be evident to all.
1 Tim 4:15

The generous soul will be made rich, and he who waters will also be watered himself.
Prov 11:25

CHARITY DRIVE

FREE TOYS

19

The goodness of God will never change.
Unlike this lollipop, God's love, His sweetness,
His goodness, His comforting ways will last forever!

…Who satisfies your mouth with good things, So that your youth is renewed like the eagle's.
Psalm 103:5

… The goodness of God endures continually.
Psalm 52:1

For His merciful kindness is great toward us, And the truth of the LORD endures forever.
Psalm 117:2

Oh, give thanks to the LORD, for He is good! For His mercy endures forever.
Psalm 136:1

Oh, taste and see that the LORD is good; Blessed is the man who trusts in Him!
Psalm 34:8

How sweet are Your words to my taste, Sweeter than honey to my mouth!
Psalm 119:103

I once asked God, "Papa, how can You be so good all the time?"
God answered, "It's just My nature Gracie, it's who I AM."

And God said to Moses, "I AM WHO I AM."
Ex 3:14
The LORD is good to all, and His tender mercies are over all His works.
Psalm 145:9

Accepting Jesus

To know love is to know Jesus. And to know Jesus is to know God the Father, because God is love. If you want to know Jesus and the Father's love, ask Him into your life. He will show you and tell you all about His love and all the gifts He has made available for you, just like He did with me. Just say;

"Jesus, I believe in my heart you are the Son of God and that you were raised from the dead and sit at the right hand of God the Father. I ask you to be my Lord and Savior. I ask you into my life and I receive my salvation now. Thank you Jesus for saving me."

Receive the Holy Spirit

If you just said that prayer and accepted Jesus into your life, or if Jesus is already part of your life, then God the Father wants to give you His Holy Spirit. The Holy Spirit will live in you and will guide you and teach you in the way of Father God. All you have to do is ask, believe and receive. Just say;

"Father, I ask for your power and your guidance to live this new life you have for me. Please fill me with your Holy Spirit. I receive Him right now. Thank you for baptizing me with your Holy Spirit."

www.ingramcontent.com/pod-product-compliance
Lightning Source LLC
Chambersburg PA
CBHW042121040426
42449CB00003B/135